friendship is …

friendship is ...

500 reasons to appreciate friends

Lisa Swerling & Ralph Lazar

CHRONICLE BOOKS

SAN FRANCISCO

4

looking ahead, together

making plans

sending each other
real mail

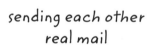

knowing you've got my back

a constant source
of inspiration

doing each other's
hair

an unexplainable connection

telling you every
little detail

wearing the same outfit
by accident

playing like kids

walking into your house
and my Wi-Fi connecting immediately

pretending to be models

sharing food on a long hike

being celebrated

Jack and Cokes

huddling up for a scary movie

standing there while you flirt

sharing heartbreak

seeing your point of view

a refuge from the storm

having the same
obsessions

a surprise call just
to say hi

a photo of
us on the fridge

a joint effort

rushing to make up

finding magic in the everyday

a crazy ride

checking out boys

a spontaneous boogie

realizing
we're reading
the same book

sharing hobbies

being equally matched

letting you show off

annoying you and thoroughly enjoying it

a movie
marathon

a warm welcome

an adventure waiting to happen

always deleting
the bad photos

telling you things you don't want to tell your self

letting you borrow
my new dress

an unsinkable boat

walking you home

laughing at our
hairstyles over
the years

Feeling closer after a
disagreement

going at the same pace

doing absolutely nothing but
having the best time

trying new foods
together

peanut butter
and jelly

being the modern
Three Musketeers

being amazed by your talent

laughing at your jokes when
they're not so good...

...and sympathizing with your
problems when they're not so bad

pulling out each other's
gray hairs

knowing all of your
embarrassing nicknames

coming to your rescue

long chats by the fire

our motley crew

remembering
something you said
and cracking up

passing notes in class

mixing your
favorite drink

a pick-up game in the park

having the same
taste in movies

Batman and Robin

cracking up for no reason

having a whole conversation
with just one look

stealing food off your plate
without you knowing

playing pool
all night long

talking sports for hours

the perfect
group picture

Harry, Hermione, and Ron

a hidden treasure

clever comebacks
to bad pick-up lines

ordering our favorite takeout

making memories

accepting your
craziness

a silly fight for
no reason

celebrating our
favorite team's win

a never-ending
online chat

a big welcome
at the airport

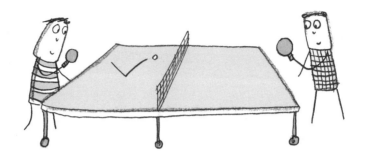

fun without words

an excuse to indulge

insisting on getting the bill

looking up old classmates

walking in when the rest of the
world has walked out

having half of your stuff at my place

finally returning all
the books I borrowed

knowing how you
take your tea

giving you a ride

working on
a project
together

being a good listener

taking you wedding dress shopping

spending holidays together

47

distracting each other

leaving for a road trip before dawn

thinking of you
when I'm away

never letting the world
get between us

a pinky promise

admiring your individuality

bringing over all the ingredients for dinner

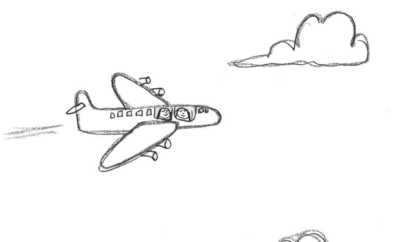

flying home for your wedding

meeting at camp and knowing
we'll be friends forever

buying a round of drinks

being in our own world

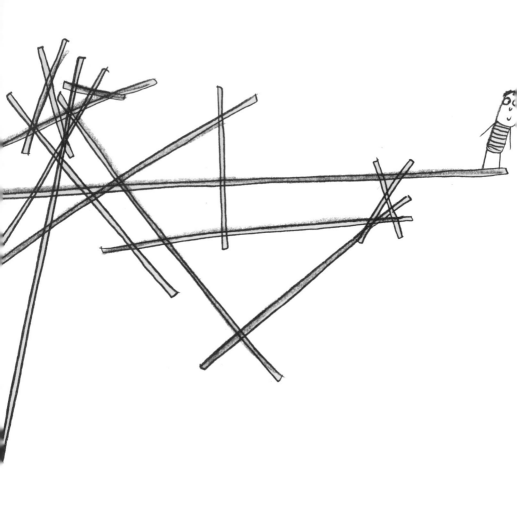

meeting halfway

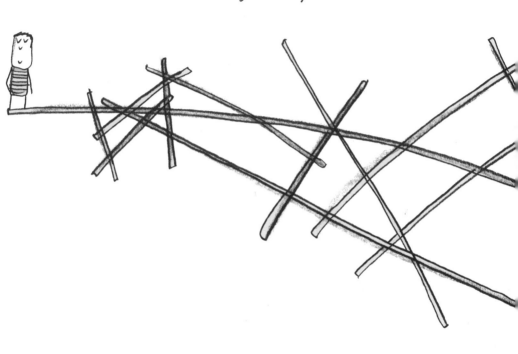

staying up talking
all night

midnight snack shopping

catching your bouquet

being neighbors

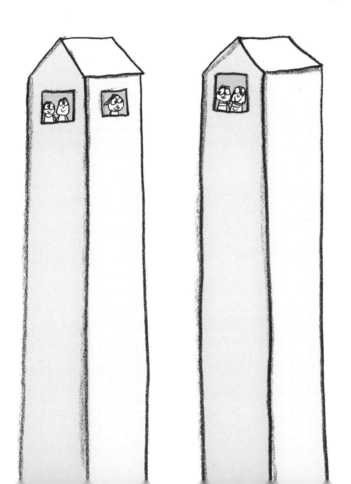

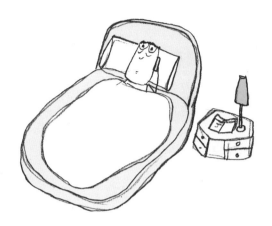

answering your call
in the middle of the night

purrfect

getting to the sale first

being in sync

going out for a drink and
staying for three

sharing a Diet Coke

a photo booth session

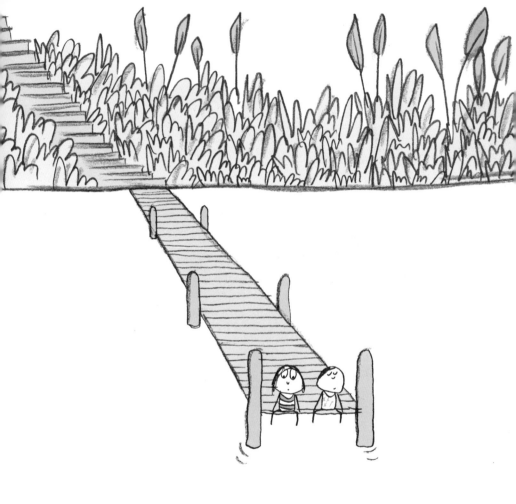

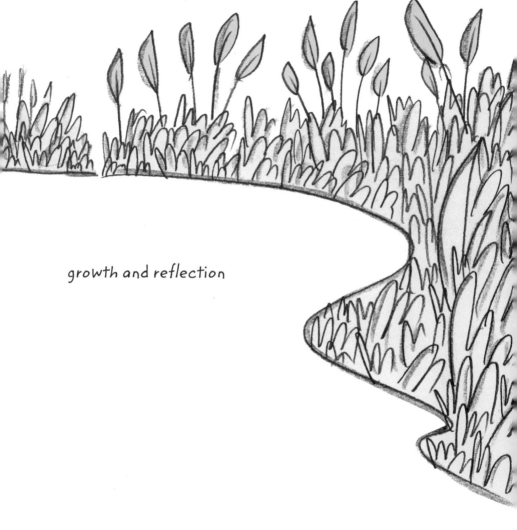

growth and reflection

you and me and
a pot of tea

having ESP

a sleepover

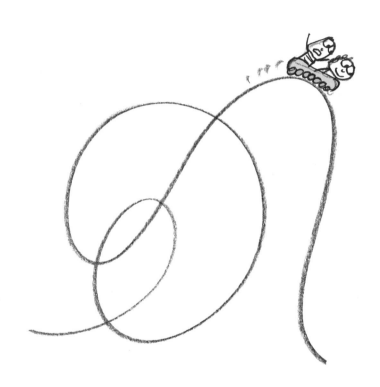

getting you to go on the fun rides

noticing that you've
lost weight

forgiving each other
no matter what

loving your children
as my own

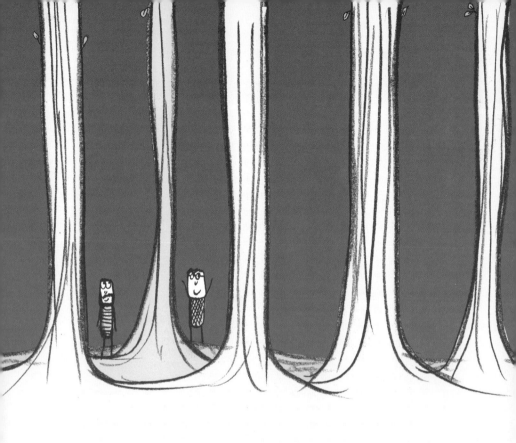

exploring together

being in tune

Joey and Chandler

solving the world's problems over dinner

tolerating your snoring

finding my other half

facing the world together

admiring your moves

crying at your wedding

reaching new heights

listening to
your tall tales

bringing out each other's funny side

sharing the last truffle

studying together
on Skype

welcoming your baby
to the world

sampling every
ice cream
flavor

a guys' weekend

  accepting the bad
with the good

toasting each other

growing separately
without growing apart

inclusive

going through our
old yearbooks

cuddling

encouraging your wildest fantasies

a bromance

sharing earphones

loaning you my
favorite books

balding at the same rate

long summer days
spent together

a sweet familiarity

helping you make
important decisions

shoe shopping

understanding your
eccentricity

empathy

moving along after an argument
as if it never happened

free therapy

playing Truth or Dare

Charlotte and Wilbur

aging gracefully together

an early morning jog through
the quiet streets

having playdates
at any age

letting you pour
your heart out

promising to marry each other
if there's no one else in the end

picking you up when you fall

the sweetest thing in life

keeping the
same beat

cheering the loudest at the game

*#$%%^

understanding all your
slang words

always finding our way
back to each other

giving honest feedback

keeping an eye on
your excesses

dropping everything
in a time of need

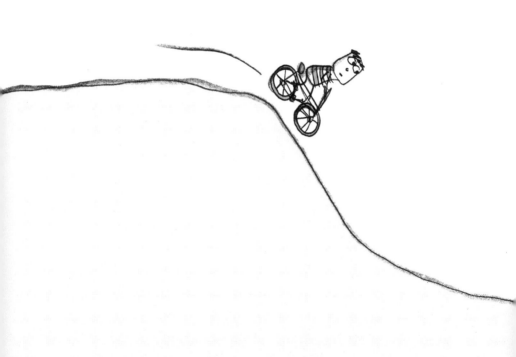

chatting and wasting time even
when we have a ton of work to do

sharing gossip
magazines

wearing each other's clothes

talking so much
we forget to eat

acting crazy in public

lip-synching into
hairbrushes

learning new
things together

sushi dates

spending *hours* at the flea market

dressing like twins

sharing the wonder of it all

having a secret language

appreciating your unique style

running through the rain

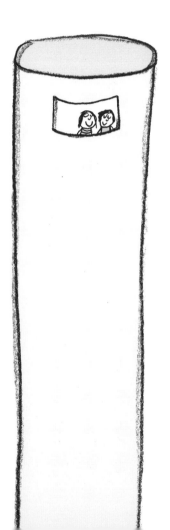

living together
in a very small place but
still liking each other

making each other
old-fashioned mix CDs

watching when you shine

having the
same shoe size

jumping on you
when you've been
away for a while

the pre-party before the actual party

watching you
unwrap my gift

laughing at our
differences

being strong for you

going on adventures

helping you
move

discovering
good music
together

sharing my happy
moments with you

inventing our own games

Laurel and Hardy

hours spent getting ready

working toward a shared goal

laughing through
everything

harmonizing

never forgetting our connection

a homemade gift

playing tricks
on you

lending a helping hand

dancing on tables

not being able to
wait to tell you stuff

finding you the perfect gift

being welcomed home

loving your laugh

taking our drinks the same way

lifelong

babysitting
your kids

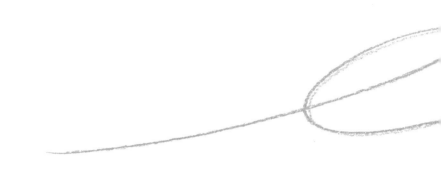

being there for special occasions

Woody & Buzz

the group you can come back to
no matter what

an excuse for a party

singing at the top of our lungs

being addicted
to the same coffee drink

constant
reassurance

a good excuse to write a letter

hand-me-downs and clothing swaps

being kindred spirits

trusting your sense
of direction

reminding each other
who we truly are

matching hairdos

calling you first
when I have
good news

making you laugh so hard
bits of cookie come out of
your nose

healthy competition

saying you look good
when you feel bad

helping you
carry your load

laughing until our
stomachs hurt

calling out in the dark and
hearing your voice

missing you
like crazy

sharing calories

spontaneity

sometimes up, sometimes down

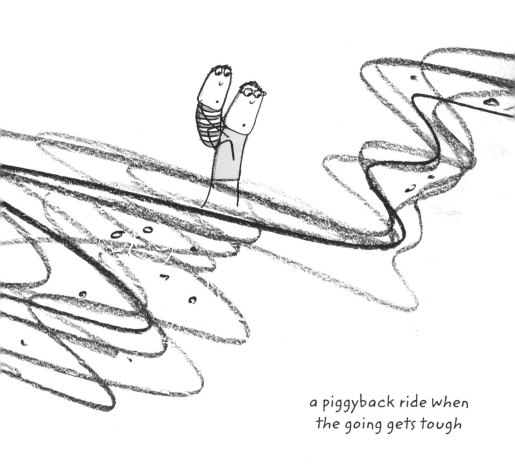

a piggyback ride when
the going gets tough

sharing childbirth
stories

looking out for
each other

being annoyed by the same people

spa days

talking total nonsense
and having that
nonsense respected

discussing the ladies

dyeing our hair

communicating solely
with emoticons

quiet companionship

teaching each
other life skills

being proud of your
achievements

showing each other the way

freedom

remembering old
camp songs

always finding
time for each other

a shared triumph

wearing the ugly
sweater you got me

camping trips

a constant
presence

overanalyzing everything

being beach babes

making your favorite meal

teamwork

chatting, chatting, chatting

good advice when I need it most

graduating at the same time

traveling together
and always feeling
right at home

building a fort

toasting nothing in
particular

finding humor in your neuroses

finding ways to see each other
no matter what

feeling as young as when we first met

going on vacation together

dragging you on boring errands to make them more fun

helping you take a leap

being excited when your crush
finally talks to you

a bear hug

food fiiight!

the best kind of
downtime

taking a selfie

not always easy

Carrie, Miranda, Charlotte,
and Samantha

understanding that
we're all just human

furry, slobbery, and
always loyal

apples & honey

asking how you are
and actually waiting
for the answer

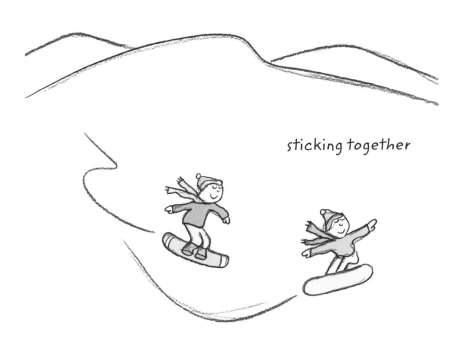

sticking together

a peaceful place, out beyond the
craziness of the world

LATE

knowing you'll
wait for me

beating you at a
board game and
rubbing it in

going to see our
favorite band

doing little favors for each other

grocery shopping for a weekend away

sharing lip gloss

having the same taste
in music

buying you flowers
for no reason

decorating each
other's homes

what keeps us afloat

navigating life

planning
tomorrow's
exploits

gossiping like schoolgirls

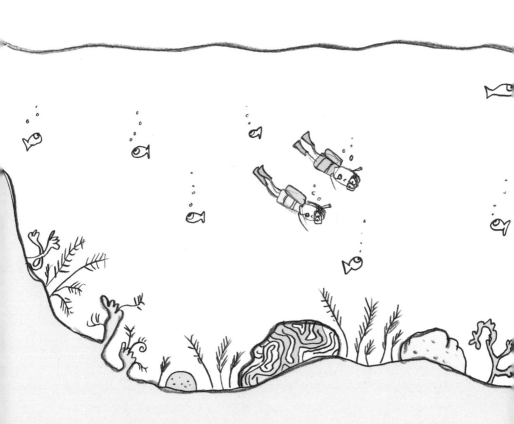

dinner party
games

comparing tan lines

still doing the things
we loved as kids

believing your dreams
will come true

sometimes messy

a light
in dark times

chill time

a soft landing

keeping a promise

fun

scratching your back
when you can't reach
the itch

clowning around

an excuse to make cocktails

bringing you soup
when you're sick

escaping from children
for a night out

a snooze in each
other's company

sharing our life histories
on the day we met

group hugs

reminding you to treat yourself

laughing uncontrollably

borrowing your
clothes and not
returning them

getting
emotional over
the same songs

laughing at your
blunders

retelling funny old stories

people asking if we're sisters

rushing to the dance floor when our song comes on

sharing one umbrella

*finding
something
special I know
you'll love*

a totally random message
at a totally random time

mustard
and ketchup

having the same conversation
over and over again, and
never getting bored

being cozy

driving cross-country

doing the total opposite
of what we'd planned

studying together
all night

synchronicity

as deep as the ocean

permission to not act our age

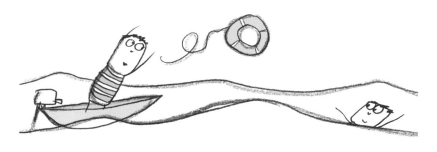

a lifesaver

forgetting all
of life's worries

sharing weird stories about
people we know

playing hooky

being the first to meet your new puppy

being each other's
date to a wedding

making you smile

making scrapbooks

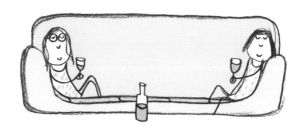

sharing a fine bottle of wine

reminding you to stay positive

group trips

grabbing your hand

riding the peaks and valleys together

defending your honor

telling each other
"You haven't
changed a bit!"

being the same
brand of weird

seeing the world
from new angles

a cold beer
on a hot day

Ben & Jerry

letting you sing out
of tune in my ear

for all seasons

knowing the pain behind
the brave face

realizing that we've been
hanging out for more than
half our lives

deep love despite
differences

an indoor picnic

racing you into the ocean

cheese and
wine

saying sorry

telling you every
detail of a date

partying like maniacs

being competitive about our facial hair

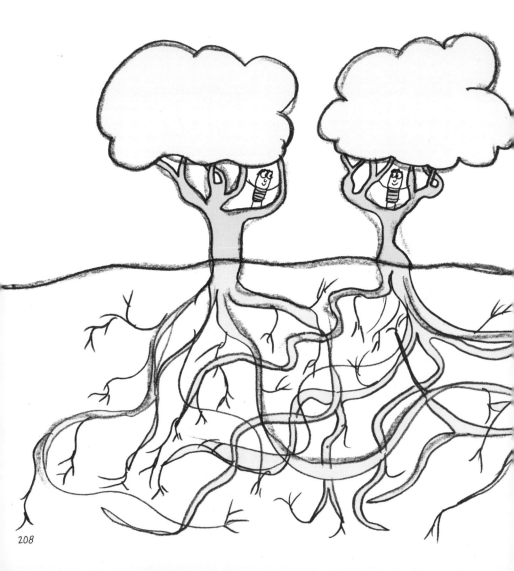

having our lives intertwined

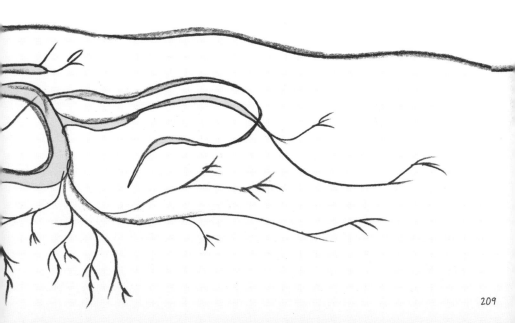

re-watching
a TV show from
our childhood

feeling your sadness
as my own

going out in our pajamas

feeling at home with
your parents

natural camaraderie

a spontaneous
gathering

being obsessed with the same team

agreeing that the scale
isn't working properly

having our own
spot in the library

making
our bucket lists

picking up the tab when you're short

being patient when
you don't feel like
socializing

having the same
sense of humor

meeting in the elevator

dreaming up names for
our future kids

texting you from
across the room

looking forward to
the same stuff

SPRING
BREAK

having an apology
accepted

being the loudest ones
in the restaurant

learning new tricks

a video game marathon

appreciating your DJ skills

meeting you at your
bus stop

trying on expensive
dresses we'll never buy

keeping my mouth shut
when you drive

impromptu visits

playing charades for hours

breaking out of the pack

flying in to see you for the weekend

knowing exactly what you'll order

a shared ride

imagining our futures

yelling "jinx!"

hanging out in your kitchen

throwing you a surprise party

sneaking fast food
now and then

taking your side even
when you're wrong

jumping in

being young at heart

pure relaxation

sneaking out of work together

helping you pack even though
I don't want you to go

being different and alike
at the same time

bumping into each other
and that being the highlight of the day

hanging out on a rainy day

 making eyes at
the same guy

 giving you the heart
of my artichoke

weekend trips to the
farmers' market

233

jamming

listening to you talk about your ex . . . again

seeing you after just a day and feeling like it's been weeks

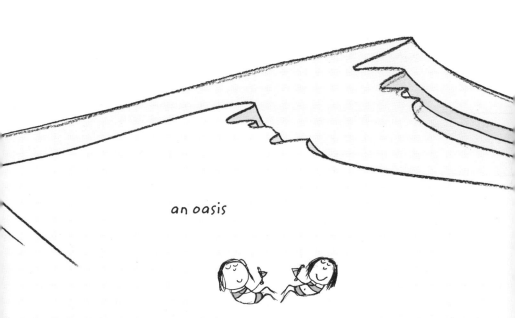

an oasis

having conversations impossible
for others to understand

knowing we'll be
troublemakers in the
nursing home one day

Sunday morning outings

making our own set of rules

trust

occasional hedonism

feeling on top of the world

traveling any distance to be by your side

sending you long, rambling emails and always getting a reply

pretzels and beer

thinking we're
funny enough to be
comedians

not minding your gross habits

remembering the foods
you don't like

helping you get a better view

243

staying in

hugging goodbye and
not wanting to let go

finishing your sentences

letting you hang on when you need to

unwavering support

convincing you to do something
spontaneous with me

having
a long history

compassion in
times of sadness

seeing the same shapes in clouds

living life to the fullest

riding the same wave

diving into
the dessert

Butch Cassidy and the Sundance Kid

the glue
that holds us
together

the good life

a question of balance

swapping secrets

knowing I can be
myself with you

dancing our worries away

an inspiring
conversation

inside jokes

having no set destination

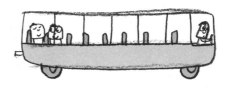

making silly videos

always having so much
to tell you

having fun no matter
where we are

our superpower

getting a text that makes me smile for the rest of the day

board game marathons

shared disappointments

being soul sisters

having the same childhood memories

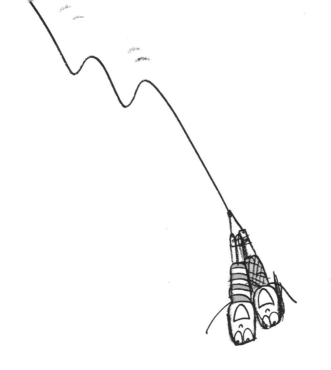

*encouraging each
other to take risks*

watching you realize your ambitions

goofing off

getting into mischief

working out our differences

a whole day of shopping

bearing some of the weight

staying out all night

calling to rehash the day
even though we were
together all day

knowing you're always
there for me

years passing and nothing
changing

having you as my ally at work

spending the whole weekend together

an impromptu BBQ

being ecstatic to find
out you're pregnant

belting out 80's hits

a night out on
the town

calling each other
names that only the
two of us know

sharing

going to the ladies' room together

hot popcorn and butter

laughing for hours over
funny online clips

the best way to end the day

quite simple, really

ISBN: 978-1-4521-3657-8

Manufactured in China

FSC
www.fsc.org
MIX
Paper from
responsible sources
FSC® C008047

Design by Lisa Swerling and Ralph Lazar

10 9 8 7 6 5 4

Chronicle Books LLC
680 Second Street
San Francisco, CA 94107
www.chroniclebooks.com